PRINCEWILL LAGANG

Innovation Mogul: Mukesh Ambani's Impact on India's Corporate Landscape

First published by PRINCEWILL LAGANG 2023

Copyright © 2023 by Princewill Lagang

All rights reserved. No part of this publication may be reproduced, stored or transmitted in any form or by any means, electronic, mechanical, photocopying, recording, scanning, or otherwise without written permission from the publisher. It is illegal to copy this book, post it to a website, or distribute it by any other means without permission.

Princewill Lagang asserts the moral right to be identified as the author of this work.

First edition

This book was professionally typeset on Reedsy.
Find out more at reedsy.com

Contents

1. Introduction — 1
2. The Genesis of a Visionary — 3
3. Pioneering Paradigms - Mukesh Ambani's Trail of Corporate... — 6
4. Redefining Sustainability - Mukesh Ambani's Green Vision — 9
5. Beyond Borders - Mukesh Ambani's Global Economic Impact — 12
6. Empowering Billions - Mukesh Ambani's Socioeconomic Legacy — 15
7. Technological Frontiers - Mukesh Ambani's Vision for the... — 18
8. Legacy of Leadership - Mukesh Ambani's Enduring Impact — 22
9. The Future Unveiled - Mukesh Ambani's Vision Beyond Tomorrow — 26
10. Beyond Business - Mukesh Ambani's Impact on Society and... — 30
11. The Unfinished Symphony - Mukesh Ambani's Ongoing Journey — 34
12. Shaping Tomorrow - Mukesh Ambani's Vision for a Global... — 38
13. The Unending Symphony - Mukesh Ambani's Enduring Legacy — 42
14. Summary — 46

1

Introduction

"Innovation Mogul: Mukesh Ambani's Impact on India's Corporate Landscape"

In the pulsating heart of India's corporate evolution, a visionary leader has emerged as a driving force behind transformative change – Mukesh Ambani. This biography delves into the life and legacy of a man whose name has become synonymous with innovation, disruption, and societal progress. Mukesh Ambani's journey, intricately woven into the fabric of India's business landscape, has not only redefined the nation's corporate identity but has reverberated globally.

Chapter by chapter, we unravel the compelling narrative of Ambani's rise, exploring the strategic brilliance that shaped Reliance Industries into a conglomerate at the forefront of technological, economic, and cultural revolutions. From the disruptive entry into telecommunications with Reliance Jio to pioneering initiatives in sustainable business practices and philanthropy, Ambani's impact extends far beyond boardrooms, leaving an indelible mark on the socio-cultural tapestry of India.

INNOVATION MOGUL: MUKESH AMBANI'S IMPACT ON INDIA'S CORPORATE LANDSCAPE

This biography transcends the traditional boundaries of business narratives, delving into Ambani's role in societal development, technological frontiers, and his vision for a sustainable future. The symphony metaphor guides us through the chapters, symbolizing the ongoing and harmonious nature of Ambani's influence.

As we embark on this journey through the life and achievements of Mukesh Ambani, we invite readers to witness the unfolding saga of an innovation mogul and his enduring legacy on the canvas of India's corporate landscape.

2

The Genesis of a Visionary

Title: "Innovation Mogul: Mukesh Ambani's Impact on India's Corporate Landscape"

The Indian sun dipped below the horizon, casting long shadows across the bustling cityscape of Mumbai. As the vibrant street markets buzzed with activity, a young Mukesh Ambani found himself captivated by the energy of entrepreneurship that permeated the air. Little did he know that this fascination would blossom into a transformative force, reshaping the very fabric of India's corporate landscape.

1.1 The Ambani Legacy

In the heart of Mumbai, where tradition and modernity coexist in a delicate dance, the Ambani family laid the foundation for a legacy that would leave an indelible mark on India's business history. Mukesh Ambani, born on April 19, 1957, into the illustrious Ambani clan, inherited not just wealth but a vision that stretched beyond conventional boundaries.

1.2 Early Years: Nurturing the Seeds of Ambition

The first whispers of Mukesh's entrepreneurial spirit were heard during his formative years. From the corridors of the University of Mumbai, where he pursued a degree in Chemical Engineering, to the familial conversations around the dinner table, the young Mukesh was exposed to the complexities and nuances of business.

1.3 Reliance Industries: A Phoenix Rises

The stage was set for Mukesh Ambani's grand entry into the corporate arena when he joined Reliance Industries, founded by his father, Dhirubhai Ambani. The company, initially a textile business, underwent a metamorphosis under Mukesh's keen business acumen.

1.3.1 Dhirubhai's Vision, Mukesh's Mission

The mantle of leadership passed from father to son, marking a pivotal moment in Reliance Industries' trajectory. Dhirubhai's audacious vision for the company found a steadfast champion in Mukesh, who saw not just a conglomerate but a vehicle for societal transformation.

1.3.2 Petrochemical Revolution

Mukesh's strategic foresight propelled Reliance into uncharted territories. The company shifted its focus to petrochemicals, revolutionizing the industry. This daring move was not merely a business decision; it was a statement of intent to position India on the global economic map.

1.4 The Telecom Revolution: Jio's Game-Changing Entry

As dusk settled over the Indian business landscape, a new dawn was on the horizon. Mukesh Ambani orchestrated one of the most significant disruptions in recent times—the launch of Jio, Reliance's telecommunications arm.

1.4.1 Democratising Connectivity

Jio's entry was more than a market move; it was a revolution aimed at bridging the digital divide. Mukesh Ambani envisioned a connected India, where every citizen, from bustling metropolises to remote villages, had access to affordable, high-speed internet.

1.4.2 Redefining Competition

The launch of Jio not only redefined the telecom sector but sent shockwaves through the entire corporate landscape. Mukesh Ambani's bold strategy of offering free trials and disruptive pricing models transformed Jio into a household name, reshaping consumer expectations and challenging competitors to innovate or fade away.

1.5 A Glimpse into the Future

As Chapter 1 unfolds the early chapters of Mukesh Ambani's journey, the stage is set for a deeper exploration of the visionary's impact on India's corporate terrain. From petrochemicals to telecommunications, Ambani's foray into diverse sectors foreshadows a trajectory marked by relentless innovation, strategic brilliance, and an unwavering commitment to shaping India's economic destiny.

In the chapters that follow, we delve deeper into the various facets of Mukesh Ambani's empire, exploring the strategies, challenges, and societal implications of his trailblazing ventures. "Innovation Mogul" is not just a biography; it is a chronicle of a man whose vision transcends boundaries, propelling India into an era of unprecedented corporate evolution.

3

Pioneering Paradigms - Mukesh Ambani's Trail of Corporate Triumphs

2.1 Diversification Dynamics

2.1.1 Beyond Petrochemicals: The Reliance Odyssey

The evolution of Reliance Industries under Mukesh Ambani was not confined to the petrochemical sector. This section unravels the strategic diversification initiatives that propelled Reliance into new realms, from refining and retail to digital services.

2.1.2 Retail Resplendence

Mukesh Ambani's foresight extended beyond conventional sectors as he steered Reliance into the retail landscape. From cornering the market with the acquisition of established retail chains to introducing innovative retail formats, Ambani's foray into this sector was nothing short of revolutionary.

2.2 Digital Disruption: The Jio Ecosystem

2.2.1 Jio Platforms: Beyond Telecommunications

Jio, originally envisioned as a telecom giant, soon morphed into an ecosystem that extended its tendrils into various digital domains. This section illuminates the strategic moves that transformed Jio into a multifaceted platform, from entertainment and e-commerce to fintech.

2.2.2 Connecting Billions: The Jio Effect

The impact of Jio's affordable internet services reached far beyond business metrics. This subsection explores how Mukesh Ambani's vision transformed the daily lives of millions, ushering in a new era of connectivity, digital inclusion, and economic empowerment.

2.3 Global Vision: Ambani's International Ventures

2.3.1 Acquisitions and Alliances

Mukesh Ambani's global vision materialized through strategic acquisitions and alliances that expanded Reliance's footprint beyond Indian borders. From energy collaborations to technological partnerships, this section unveils the international dimension of Ambani's corporate strategy.

2.3.2 Challenges and Triumphs Abroad

While expanding globally, Ambani encountered challenges unique to international markets. Explore how he navigated cultural nuances, regulatory landscapes, and global competition, turning obstacles into opportunities.

2.4 The Man Behind the Mogul: Mukesh Ambani's Leadership Style

2.4.1 Visionary Leadership

This section delves into the leadership philosophy that guided Mukesh Ambani's decisions. From fostering innovation to nurturing a culture of excellence, Ambani's leadership style goes beyond business strategies, reflecting a commitment to societal progress.

2.4.2 Challenges and Criticisms

No corporate journey is without its share of challenges and criticisms. Uncover the storms Mukesh Ambani weathered, from regulatory scrutiny to public skepticism, and how he emerged from these trials with his vision intact.

2.5 Shaping the Future: Mukesh Ambani's Vision for Tomorrow

As Chapter 2 draws to a close, a glimpse into Mukesh Ambani's future unfolds. From green energy initiatives to cutting-edge technological pursuits, explore the projects and ambitions that signify Ambani's enduring commitment to innovation and the continued transformation of India's corporate landscape. "Pioneering Paradigms" not only captures the milestones of Mukesh Ambani's journey but sets the stage for the unfolding chapters of an extraordinary corporate saga.

4

Redefining Sustainability - Mukesh Ambani's Green Vision

3.1 The Green Imperative

3.1.1 Environmental Consciousness: A Paradigm Shift

Mukesh Ambani's journey takes a conscientious turn as he spearheads the charge towards sustainability. This section unravels the pivotal moments that led to Ambani's awakening to the environmental challenges and his commitment to integrating sustainability into the core of his corporate empire.

3.1.2 From Petrochemicals to Green Energy

Trace the transformative steps as Mukesh Ambani, once synonymous with the petrochemical industry, redirects his focus toward renewable energy. The chapter explores Reliance Industries' foray into green initiatives, from solar and wind energy projects to sustainable technologies.

3.2 Project New Horizons: Ambani's Green Energy Ambitions

3.2.1 Solar Power Revolution

Under Ambani's leadership, Reliance Industries emerges as a trailblazer in the solar power sector. Dive into the details of ambitious solar projects, their impact on India's energy landscape, and the global implications of Mukesh Ambani's green vision.

3.2.2 Wind Energy Ventures

Wind energy becomes a cornerstone of Mukesh Ambani's sustainable agenda. This subsection illuminates the strategic decisions, technological innovations, and partnerships that mark Reliance's footprint in harnessing wind power for a greener tomorrow.

3.3 The Circular Economy Commitment

3.3.1 Waste to Wealth: Reliance's Circular Economy Initiatives

Mukesh Ambani's commitment to sustainability extends beyond energy. Explore how Reliance Industries navigates the challenges of waste management, transforming them into opportunities through innovative solutions and circular economy principles.

3.3.2 Ethical Sourcing and Responsible Practices

Uncover the ethical dimensions of Ambani's sustainability drive. This section delves into the emphasis on responsible sourcing, fair labor practices, and corporate social responsibility that define Reliance's commitment to creating a sustainable and socially conscious business ecosystem.

3.4 Challenges and Triumphs in Sustainability

3.4.1 Regulatory Hurdles and Public Perception

Mukesh Ambani's pivot to sustainability is not without obstacles. Examine the regulatory challenges, public expectations, and the delicate balance Ambani must maintain as he navigates the uncharted waters of sustainable business practices.

3.4.2 Triumphs of Innovation

Highlighting the triumphs of innovation, this subsection explores how Mukesh Ambani's commitment to sustainability transforms challenges into opportunities, setting new benchmarks for the corporate world and inspiring a generation of eco-conscious leaders.

3.5 Beyond Business: Mukesh Ambani's Global Environmental Advocacy

3.5.1 The Global Impact of Reliance's Green Initiatives

Mukesh Ambani's environmental advocacy extends beyond the borders of India. This section showcases how Reliance's green initiatives contribute to global sustainability efforts, influencing industry practices and challenging the status quo.

3.5.2 Collaborative Sustainability: Ambani's Call to Action

As Chapter 3 concludes, the narrative shifts from corporate endeavors to a broader call for collaborative action. Mukesh Ambani's green vision transcends individual success, emphasizing the collective responsibility of corporations to safeguard the planet. "Redefining Sustainability" not only explores Ambani's eco-centric evolution but prompts reflection on the role of business in mitigating environmental challenges for a sustainable future.

5

Beyond Borders - Mukesh Ambani's Global Economic Impact

4.1 The Globalization Gambit

4.1.1 Reliance's International Expansion

Mukesh Ambani's vision extends far beyond the shores of India as he strategically positions Reliance Industries on the global stage. This section unravels the motives, challenges, and triumphs of Reliance's international expansion, from market penetration to establishing a global presence.

4.1.2 Economic Diplomacy: Ambani's Role in India's Global Image

Explore Mukesh Ambani's role as an economic diplomat, influencing not just corporate landscapes but contributing to India's perception in the global economic arena. From trade partnerships to collaborations, Ambani becomes a key player in shaping India's economic narrative.

4.2 Silicon Valley Sojourn: Reliance's Tech Odyssey

4.2.1 Investments in Tech Giants

Mukesh Ambani's strategic investments in Silicon Valley redefine the contours of Reliance Industries. This section explores the partnerships and acquisitions that position Reliance as a significant player in the global technology landscape, impacting industries from telecommunications to cutting-edge innovation.

4.2.2 The Tech-Driven Future: Reliance's Vision for the Digital Age

Delve into Mukesh Ambani's foresight as he positions Reliance at the forefront of the digital revolution. From artificial intelligence to blockchain, this subsection explores how Ambani's technological pursuits not only influence global markets but anticipate the future of business.

4.3 Economic Resilience: Navigating Global Challenges

4.3.1 Global Economic Shifts: The Ambani Approach

Explore how Mukesh Ambani's economic strategies navigate the complexities of global economic shifts. From financial crises to geopolitical challenges, Ambani's resilience and adaptability become pillars of Reliance Industries' success.

4.3.2 Weathering the Storms: Lessons from Economic Downturns

Uncover how Reliance Industries, under Ambani's stewardship, weathers economic downturns. This section examines the strategies deployed to navigate recessions and crises, turning adversity into opportunities for growth.

4.4 Human Capital on a Global Scale

4.4.1 Talent Acquisition Strategies

Mukesh Ambani's global ambitions are mirrored in the talent he attracts. This subsection explores how Reliance Industries strategically acquires and nurtures a diverse pool of global talent, contributing to its status as a hub for innovation and excellence.

4.4.2 Corporate Culture Across Continents

Delve into the intricacies of Reliance's corporate culture as it transcends geographical boundaries. From fostering diversity and inclusion to instilling a sense of shared purpose, Ambani's influence on corporate culture becomes a key factor in the global success of Reliance Industries.

4.5 The Road Ahead: Ambani's Vision for Global Impact

4.5.1 Sustainable Globalization

As Chapter 4 draws to a close, the narrative shifts to Mukesh Ambani's vision for the future of Reliance Industries on the global stage. From sustainable business practices to ethical globalization, Ambani's roadmap sets the course for a corporate future that transcends borders and fosters a global community.

"Beyond Borders" not only chronicles Mukesh Ambani's impact on the global economic landscape but sets the stage for the unfolding chapters of Reliance Industries' journey into uncharted territories, guided by a visionary leader with a relentless commitment to excellence and innovation.

6

Empowering Billions - Mukesh Ambani's Socioeconomic Legacy

5.1 Corporate Social Responsibility: A Moral Imperative

5.1.1 Foundations of Giving: Reliance's Early CSR Initiatives

Explore the roots of Mukesh Ambani's commitment to corporate social responsibility (CSR). This section traces the early philanthropic endeavors of Reliance Industries and Ambani's belief in using corporate success as a catalyst for positive societal change.

5.1.2 Expanding Horizons: Reliance Foundation

Witness the evolution of Reliance Foundation, the philanthropic arm of Reliance Industries. From healthcare and education to rural development, this subsection delves into the multifaceted initiatives aimed at uplifting communities and fostering sustainable development.

5.2 Revolutionizing Education: Ambani's Educational Vision

5.2.1 Affordable and Accessible Education

Mukesh Ambani's commitment to education takes center stage as Reliance Industries pioneers initiatives to make quality education accessible to all. Explore the innovative approaches that Ambani adopts to revolutionize the education sector and empower the youth.

5.2.2 Digital Learning Initiatives

As technology becomes an integral part of education, this section explores Mukesh Ambani's endeavors to leverage digital platforms for learning. From online courses to digital literacy programs, Ambani's vision extends beyond traditional educational boundaries.

5.3 Healthcare for All: Ambani's Medical Missions

5.3.1 Reliance Hospitals: A Network of Healing

Dive into the healthcare initiatives spearheaded by Mukesh Ambani. This subsection outlines the establishment and expansion of Reliance Hospitals, providing quality healthcare services and contributing to the well-being of communities across India.

5.3.2 Rural Healthcare Outreach

Ambani's vision for healthcare transcends urban centers. Explore how Reliance Foundation takes healthcare to rural India, addressing the unique challenges of remote areas and promoting preventive care to improve the overall health of the nation.

5.4 Rural Empowerment: Ambani's Agrarian Initiatives

5.4.1 Agriculture and Farmer Welfare

Witness Mukesh Ambani's commitment to rural empowerment and agricultural development. This section explores initiatives aimed at improving farming practices, ensuring fair prices for farmers, and fostering sustainability in the agricultural sector.

5.4.2 Rural Entrepreneurship Programs

Ambani's vision for rural empowerment extends beyond agriculture. Discover how Reliance Foundation supports and nurtures rural entrepreneurship, creating opportunities for individuals in rural communities to become self-reliant and contribute to economic growth.

5.5 Social Impact Metrics: Evaluating Success Beyond Profit

5.5.1 Measuring Impact: The Reliance Approach

As corporate social responsibility becomes an integral part of Reliance Industries, this section explores the methodologies used to measure and evaluate the social impact of Ambani's initiatives, emphasizing transparency and accountability.

5.5.2 Lessons for the Corporate World

As Chapter 5 concludes, the narrative expands beyond Mukesh Ambani's socioeconomic initiatives to extract lessons for the broader corporate world. Ambani's legacy becomes a case study in the symbiotic relationship between corporate success and social responsibility, offering a blueprint for businesses seeking to make a meaningful impact on society.

"Empowering Billions" not only highlights Mukesh Ambani's commitment to socioeconomic development but underscores the transformative power of corporations to be agents of positive change in the world.

7

Technological Frontiers - Mukesh Ambani's Vision for the Future

6.1 The Digital Revolution Unleashed

6.1.1 5G Ambitions: Redefining Connectivity

Mukesh Ambani's relentless pursuit of technological excellence takes center stage as Reliance Industries sets its sights on 5G technology. Explore how Ambani envisions a future where high-speed, reliable connectivity becomes the bedrock for transformative innovations across industries.

6.1.2 Internet of Things (IoT): Connecting the Unconnected

Delve into Ambani's vision for the Internet of Things and its potential to reshape industries and daily life. From smart cities to connected devices, this section explores how Reliance Industries positions itself at the forefront of the IoT revolution.

6.2 Artificial Intelligence and Beyond

6.2.1 AI Integration: Shaping Industries

Mukesh Ambani's foray into artificial intelligence becomes a linchpin in Reliance's technological arsenal. Uncover how AI applications are reshaping industries, from manufacturing and healthcare to finance, as Ambani propels Reliance into the vanguard of the Fourth Industrial Revolution.

6.2.2 Ethical AI: Ambani's Guiding Principles

Explore Mukesh Ambani's commitment to ethical AI practices. This subsection examines the principles guiding Reliance Industries in the responsible development and deployment of artificial intelligence, ensuring that technology serves humanity without compromising ethical standards.

6.3 E-Commerce Ambitions

6.3.1 Digital Marketplaces: Redefining Retail

Ambani's vision for the future extends to the realm of e-commerce. Trace the strategic moves and innovative approaches as Reliance Industries establishes itself as a major player in digital marketplaces, reshaping the landscape of online retail.

6.3.2 Integration of Online and Offline Retail

Delve into the convergence of online and offline retail strategies. This section explores how Ambani's vision combines the convenience of e-commerce with the experiential aspect of physical stores, creating a seamless and customer-centric retail ecosystem.

6.4 Quantum Computing and Cutting-Edge Technologies

6.4.1 Quantum Leap: Reliance's Quantum Computing Initiatives

Explore Mukesh Ambani's ventures into quantum computing and other cutting-edge technologies. This subsection unveils how Reliance Industries is positioning itself at the forefront of technological advancements that have the potential to revolutionize computation and problem-solving.

6.4.2 Collaboration for Innovation

As technological frontiers expand, Ambani's approach to collaboration becomes instrumental. Discover how Reliance Industries fosters partnerships with research institutions, startups, and global tech leaders to drive innovation and stay ahead in the rapidly evolving technological landscape.

6.5 Challenges and Ethical Considerations

6.5.1 Technological Challenges and Regulatory Scrutiny

With great technological leaps come great challenges. This section explores the obstacles and regulatory scrutiny that Ambani's technological ventures encounter and how Reliance Industries navigates these complexities to stay on the cutting edge.

6.5.2 Ethical Dilemmas in the Tech Space

Examine the ethical considerations that arise in the development and deployment of advanced technologies. Mukesh Ambani's commitment to ethical practices is put to the test as Reliance Industries pioneers innovations that have far-reaching implications for society.

6.6 Visionaries of Tomorrow: Ambani's Legacy in Technology

6.6.1 Fostering the Next Generation of Innovators

As Chapter 6 concludes, the focus shifts to Mukesh Ambani's vision for nurturing the next generation of technological visionaries. Explore how Reliance Industries invests in education, research, and mentorship programs to cultivate a talent pool that will continue pushing the boundaries of innovation.

"Technological Frontiers" not only unveils Mukesh Ambani's current technological pursuits but sets the stage for the next chapter of Reliance Industries' journey into uncharted territories, guided by a visionary leader with an unwavering commitment to staying at the forefront of technological innovation.

8

Legacy of Leadership - Mukesh Ambani's Enduring Impact

7.1 Leadership in Flux: The Evolution of Mukesh Ambani's Style

7.1.1 Adapting to Change: Ambani's Leadership Evolution

Witness the evolution of Mukesh Ambani's leadership style over the years. This section explores how Ambani adapts to changing business landscapes, emerging technologies, and evolving global dynamics while remaining steadfast in his commitment to innovation and excellence.

7.1.2 Leadership in Crisis: Navigating Uncharted Waters

Examine Mukesh Ambani's prowess in crisis management. From economic downturns to global pandemics, this subsection delves into how Ambani's leadership steers Reliance Industries through turbulent times, ensuring resilience and sustainable growth.

7.2 Visionary Stewardship: Shaping Industries

7.2.1 Industries Transformed: Ambani's Impact

Explore the far-reaching impact of Mukesh Ambani's vision on various industries. From petrochemicals and telecommunications to technology and sustainability, this section examines how Ambani's strategies have reshaped traditional sectors and forged new frontiers.

7.2.2 Global Influence: Ambani's Contribution to the World Economy

Delve into Ambani's influence on the global economy. This subsection explores how Reliance Industries, under Ambani's leadership, has become a key player in shaping economic trends, trade relationships, and global business paradigms.

7.3 Ambani's Socioeconomic Legacy

7.3.1 Empowering Communities: Socioeconomic Impact

Reflect on Mukesh Ambani's contributions to societal development. From education and healthcare to rural empowerment, this section analyzes how Ambani's philanthropic endeavors have left an indelible mark on communities across India.

7.3.2 Lessons for Corporate Social Responsibility

Extract lessons from Ambani's CSR initiatives. As the corporate world grapples with its role in societal development, Ambani's legacy becomes a blueprint for integrating corporate success with meaningful contributions to social welfare.

7.4 Technological Pioneer and Innovator

7.4.1 Technological Legacy: Ambani's Impact on Innovation

Assess Mukesh Ambani's legacy as a technological pioneer. This subsection explores the enduring impact of Ambani's ventures in areas like 5G, artificial intelligence, and quantum computing, influencing the trajectory of technological advancement.

7.4.2 Shaping the Digital Future

Uncover Ambani's role in shaping the digital future. From telecommunications to e-commerce and beyond, this section examines how Reliance Industries, under Ambani's guidance, has become a force driving the digital transformation of industries and societies.

7.5 Challenges and Reflections

7.5.1 Navigating Controversies

Examine the controversies and challenges that Mukesh Ambani and Reliance Industries have faced. This section explores how Ambani navigates controversies with resilience and how these experiences contribute to the ongoing evolution of his leadership.

7.5.2 Reflections on a Storied Career

As Chapter 7 concludes, take a moment to reflect on Mukesh Ambani's storied career. This section explores Ambani's reflections on the journey, the lessons learned, and his vision for the future as he continues to lead Reliance Industries into a new era.

7.6 The Unfolding Legacy

7.6.1 The Next Chapter: Ambani's Vision for the Future

The narrative concludes with Mukesh Ambani's vision for the future.

From sustainability initiatives and technological innovations to global collaborations, explore the roadmap that Ambani envisions for Reliance Industries and his lasting legacy in the annals of business history.

"Legacy of Leadership" not only encapsulates the milestones of Mukesh Ambani's journey but serves as a testament to the enduring impact of a visionary leader who has not only transformed industries but has also left an indelible mark on the global business landscape.

9

The Future Unveiled - Mukesh Ambani's Vision Beyond Tomorrow

8.1 Navigating Uncharted Territories

8.1.1 The Ever-Evolving Landscape

As Mukesh Ambani continues to lead Reliance Industries into the future, this section explores the dynamic nature of the business landscape and Ambani's strategies for navigating uncharted territories. From emerging technologies to global economic shifts, discover how Ambani anticipates and adapts to change.

8.1.2 Beyond Industries: Ambani's Interdisciplinary Approach

Witness Mukesh Ambani's interdisciplinary approach to business. This subsection delves into how Ambani envisions the convergence of industries, creating synergies that redefine traditional boundaries and foster innovation on a scale previously unimagined.

8.2 The Green Revolution: Scaling Sustainable Heights

8.2.1 Ambani's Commitment to Green Energy

Explore Ambani's unwavering commitment to sustainable practices. This section unfolds the next phase of Reliance Industries' green revolution, from ambitious renewable energy projects to eco-friendly initiatives that position the conglomerate as a global leader in sustainability.

8.2.2 Circular Economy Champions: Ambani's Pledge

Delve into how Ambani takes the circular economy commitment further. From waste reduction to resource efficiency, this subsection explores how Reliance Industries is pioneering circular economy practices that set benchmarks for the industry.

8.3 Technological Marvels: Beyond the Horizon

8.3.1 Cutting-Edge Technologies on the Horizon

Explore the technological marvels that Ambani envisions for the future. From advancements in artificial intelligence and quantum computing to disruptive innovations in e-commerce and telecommunications, this section paints a picture of the next wave of technological revolutions led by Reliance Industries.

8.3.2 Ethical Tech: A Pillar of the Future

Examine Ambani's emphasis on ethical technology. As the world grapples with the ethical implications of technological advancements, this subsection explores how Ambani aims to ensure that Reliance Industries remains at the forefront of innovation while upholding ethical standards.

8.4 Global Collaborations and Partnerships

8.4.1 Forging Alliances: Ambani's Global Collaborations

Uncover how Mukesh Ambani continues to forge alliances with global leaders and organizations. This section explores partnerships that transcend borders, contributing to the mutual growth and success of Reliance Industries and its collaborators.

8.4.2 Diplomacy Through Business: Ambani's Role in Global Relations

Explore the role of Ambani as a key player in economic diplomacy. From trade agreements to international collaborations, this subsection delves into how Ambani's leadership contributes to strengthening global relations through business initiatives.

8.5 Shaping the Next Generation of Leaders

8.5.1 Mentorship and Education Initiatives

Witness Ambani's commitment to nurturing the next generation of leaders. This section explores mentorship programs, educational initiatives, and strategies employed by Reliance Industries to cultivate a talent pool that will carry forward the legacy of innovation and leadership.

8.5.2 Leadership Lessons: Ambani's Legacy of Mentorship

Reflect on the leadership lessons imparted by Mukesh Ambani. Through mentorship and guidance, Ambani shapes a legacy of leadership that extends beyond his tenure, leaving an indelible mark on the ethos of Reliance Industries and the leaders of tomorrow.

8.6 A Visionary's Reflections

8.6.1 Mukesh Ambani's Personal Reflections

As Chapter 8 concludes, the narrative shifts to Mukesh Ambani's personal reflections on the journey so far and the vision for the future. This section provides insights into Ambani's thoughts on leadership, innovation, and the legacy he aspires to leave behind.

"The Future Unveiled" not only provides a glimpse into Mukesh Ambani's vision beyond tomorrow but sets the stage for the unfolding chapters of Reliance Industries' journey into a future guided by a visionary leader with an unwavering commitment to excellence, sustainability, and technological innovation.

10

Beyond Business - Mukesh Ambani's Impact on Society and Culture

9.1 Cultural Catalyst: Ambani's Role in Shaping Indian Society

9.1.1 The Ambani Effect on Cultural Shifts

Explore how Mukesh Ambani's influence extends beyond the corporate realm, shaping societal norms and cultural dynamics in India. This section delves into Ambani's impact on lifestyle, consumer behavior, and the evolving aspirations of the Indian populace.

9.1.2 The Ambani Family: Icons of Modern India

Examine the public perception of the Ambani family as cultural icons. From high-profile events to philanthropic endeavors, this subsection explores how the Ambani family's visibility contributes to the evolving narrative of modern India.

9.2 Sporting Ambitions: Ambani's Foray into Sports

9.2.1 Reliance Foundation's Sports Initiatives

Dive into Mukesh Ambani's contributions to the sports landscape. From grassroots development to professional leagues, this section explores how Reliance Foundation's sports initiatives aim to foster talent, promote fitness, and contribute to the overall well-being of the nation.

9.2.2 The IPL Revolution: Reliance and Cricket

Uncover Ambani's role in revolutionizing Indian cricket through the Indian Premier League (IPL). This subsection explores how Reliance Industries' association with the IPL not only transforms the cricketing landscape but also becomes a cultural phenomenon with a global impact.

9.3 Philanthropy Beyond Borders

9.3.1 Global Humanitarian Contributions

Explore how Mukesh Ambani's philanthropic efforts extend beyond national boundaries. This section unveils Reliance Foundation's global initiatives, contributing to humanitarian causes, disaster relief, and sustainable development in collaboration with international organizations.

9.3.2 Cultural Exchange and Global Understanding

Examine Ambani's role in fostering cultural exchange and global understanding through philanthropy. From art and education to healthcare, discover how Reliance Industries' cultural initiatives contribute to building bridges and fostering mutual respect on the global stage.

9.4 Media Influence: Ambani's Presence in the Public Sphere

9.4.1 Reliance and Media Ventures

Explore Mukesh Ambani's influence on the media landscape. From ownership of major media outlets to strategic investments in digital platforms, this subsection delves into how Reliance Industries shapes narratives, disseminates information, and engages with the public through various media channels.

9.4.2 Navigating Media Challenges

Examine how Ambani navigates challenges and criticisms in the media. From controversies to public scrutiny, this section explores the strategies employed by Reliance Industries to maintain a positive public image and transparency in its media engagements.

9.5 Cultural Sustainability: Preserving Heritage and Arts

9.5.1 Reliance's Initiatives in Cultural Preservation

Explore Mukesh Ambani's endeavors in cultural sustainability. From supporting traditional arts and crafts to preserving heritage sites, this section highlights Reliance Industries' commitment to fostering a sense of cultural pride and continuity.

9.5.2 Arts and Innovation: Reliance Cultural Centers

Delve into the role of Reliance Cultural Centers in promoting arts and innovation. This subsection explores how these centers become hubs for artistic expression, cultural events, and collaborative initiatives that enrich the cultural fabric of communities.

9.6 The Future of Cultural Impact

9.6.1 Mukesh Ambani's Vision for Cultural Influence

As Chapter 9 concludes, the narrative shifts to Mukesh Ambani's vision for the future of cultural impact. This section explores Ambani's aspirations for Reliance Industries to continue playing a pivotal role in shaping societal values, fostering cultural vibrancy, and contributing to a progressive and inclusive society.

"Beyond Business" not only captures the multifaceted impact of Mukesh Ambani on society and culture but sets the stage for the continued evolution of Reliance Industries as a cultural catalyst and a force for positive change in the world.

11

The Unfinished Symphony - Mukesh Ambani's Ongoing Journey

10.1 Uncharted Horizons: Reliance's Ongoing Expansion

10.1.1 Diversification Strategies

Explore how Mukesh Ambani continues to lead Reliance Industries into new realms. From traditional industries to emerging sectors, this section delves into the ongoing diversification strategies that shape the conglomerate's portfolio and its impact on the global business landscape.

10.1.2 Innovations Across Industries

Uncover the latest innovations and technological advancements spearheaded by Reliance Industries. From cutting-edge developments in artificial intelligence to sustainable practices in manufacturing, this subsection explores how Ambani's commitment to innovation continues to drive the company's success.

10.2 Global Footprint: Reliance's Presence Around the World

10.2.1 International Ventures and Collaborations

Explore Reliance Industries' continued expansion beyond Indian borders. This section unveils ongoing international ventures, collaborations, and strategic alliances that contribute to the globalization of Reliance Industries under Ambani's leadership.

10.2.2 Challenges and Triumphs Abroad

Examine the challenges faced by Reliance Industries in the international arena and how Mukesh Ambani navigates these hurdles. From regulatory complexities to market dynamics, this subsection provides insights into the strategies employed to ensure success on a global scale.

10.3 Sustainable Futures: Reliance's Ongoing Green Revolution

10.3.1 Scaling Green Energy Initiatives

Delve into the latest developments in Reliance Industries' green initiatives. From renewable energy projects to advancements in sustainable technologies, this section explores how Ambani's vision for a greener future continues to shape the company's trajectory.

10.3.2 Circular Economy Excellence

Explore ongoing initiatives that exemplify Reliance Industries' commitment to the circular economy. This subsection examines how the conglomerate continues to pioneer solutions for waste reduction, resource efficiency, and responsible business practices.

10.4 Technological Frontiers: Ambani's Continued Pursuit of Innovation

10.4.1 The Next Wave of Technological Advancements

Explore the latest technological frontiers Ambani is venturing into. From exploring quantum computing to pushing the boundaries of artificial intelligence, this section unravels ongoing projects that position Reliance Industries at the forefront of technological innovation.

10.4.2 Ethical Tech Practices

Examine how Ambani and Reliance Industries address ethical considerations in the ever-evolving tech landscape. This subsection explores ongoing efforts to ensure that technological advancements align with ethical standards and societal well-being.

10.5 Legacy Building: The Next Chapter

10.5.1 Leadership Transition Plans

As Mukesh Ambani continues his journey, explore the evolving landscape of leadership within Reliance Industries. This section provides insights into leadership transition plans and the cultivation of a new generation of leaders to carry forward Ambani's vision.

10.5.2 The Enduring Impact of Mukesh Ambani

Reflect on the enduring impact Mukesh Ambani has had on Reliance Industries and the broader business landscape. This subsection examines the legacy Ambani is shaping and the principles that will continue to guide the company in the years to come.

10.6 The Symphony Continues: Ambani's Ongoing Vision

10.6.1 Mukesh Ambani's Continued Vision

As Chapter 10 draws to a close, the narrative shifts to Mukesh Ambani's continued vision for Reliance Industries. From the pursuit of excellence to a commitment to societal progress, this section provides a glimpse into the ongoing symphony Ambani is conducting in the business world.

"The Unfinished Symphony" not only encapsulates the ongoing journey of Mukesh Ambani but sets the stage for the future chapters of Reliance Industries' evolving saga—a saga guided by a visionary leader with an unwavering commitment to innovation, sustainability, and shaping a positive impact on the world.

12

Shaping Tomorrow - Mukesh Ambani's Vision for a Global Future

11.1 Global Leadership: Reliance Industries on the World Stage

11.1.1 Reliance Industries as a Global Force

Explore how Mukesh Ambani envisions Reliance Industries as a global leader across industries. This section delves into the strategies employed to strengthen the company's global presence, foster international collaborations, and contribute to the global economy.

11.1.2 Shaping Global Trade and Economics

Examine Ambani's role in shaping global trade and economic policies. From trade agreements to economic partnerships, this subsection explores how Reliance Industries, under Ambani's leadership, becomes an influential player in the global economic arena.

11.2 Technological Utopia: Ambani's Vision for the Digital Future

11.2.1 The Next Digital Frontier

Delve into Ambani's vision for the next digital frontier. From advancements in 6G technology to breakthroughs in quantum computing, this section explores how Reliance Industries is poised to lead the charge in defining the technological landscape of the future.

11.2.2 Democratizing Technology: Access for All

Explore how Ambani envisions technology as a democratizing force. This subsection examines initiatives aimed at ensuring that technological advancements are accessible to all, bridging the digital divide and fostering inclusive progress on a global scale.

11.3 Global Sustainability Imperative

11.3.1 A Blueprint for Sustainable Business

Examine Ambani's blueprint for embedding sustainability into global business practices. From reducing carbon footprints to fostering circular economies, this section explores how Reliance Industries contributes to the global sustainability imperative.

11.3.2 Collaborative Solutions for Global Challenges

Explore how Ambani advocates for collaborative solutions to global challenges. From climate change to social inequality, this subsection unveils initiatives that showcase Reliance Industries' commitment to working with global partners to address pressing issues.

11.4 Cultural Diplomacy: Reliance Industries as a Cultural Ambassador

11.4.1 Reliance's Cultural Diplomacy Initiatives

Dive into cultural diplomacy initiatives led by Reliance Industries. From supporting cultural exchange programs to preserving global heritage, this section explores how Ambani envisions the company as a cultural ambassador fostering understanding and appreciation among diverse societies.

11.4.2 Arts, Sports, and Shared Humanity

Examine how Ambani uses arts, sports, and shared cultural experiences to bridge gaps and build connections globally. This subsection explores the role of cultural initiatives in promoting a sense of shared humanity and fostering goodwill on the international stage.

11.5 The Ethical Corporation: A Global Model

11.5.1 Reliance's Ethical Business Practices

Explore how Ambani sets Reliance Industries as a global model for ethical business practices. From fair labor standards to transparent corporate governance, this section delves into initiatives that position the company as a beacon of ethical corporate behavior.

11.5.2 Corporate Social Responsibility Without Borders

Examine Ambani's vision for corporate social responsibility without borders. This subsection explores how Reliance Industries extends its philanthropic endeavors globally, contributing to societal development and humanitarian causes beyond national boundaries.

11.6 A Visionary's Reflection on a Global Legacy

11.6.1 Mukesh Ambani's Reflections on a Global Journey

As Chapter 11 concludes, the narrative shifts to Mukesh Ambani's personal reflections on shaping a global future. This section provides insights into Ambani's thoughts on leadership, collaboration, and the legacy he aspires to leave on a global scale.

"Shaping Tomorrow" not only envisions Mukesh Ambani's global leadership but sets the stage for Reliance Industries' role as a transformative force in defining a future where technology, sustainability, and cultural understanding converge on the global stage.

13

The Unending Symphony - Mukesh Ambani's Enduring Legacy

12.1 Continuity of Vision: Mukesh Ambani's Stewardship

12.1.1 Passing the Baton: Leadership Continuity

Explore the plans for leadership continuity within Reliance Industries. From succession strategies to the cultivation of a leadership pipeline, this section provides insights into how Mukesh Ambani envisions the seamless transition of leadership to ensure the continuity of his vision.

12.1.2 Stewardship Principles: Guiding the Next Generation

Delve into the principles that will guide the next generation of leaders within Reliance Industries. This subsection explores the values, ethics, and visionary principles that will serve as the foundation for the company's continued success.

12.2 Sustaining Excellence: Reliance Industries in Perpetuity

12.2.1 Perpetual Innovation: A Cultural Imperative

Explore how innovation becomes ingrained in the culture of Reliance Industries. From research and development to fostering a culture of continuous improvement, this section delves into the strategies for sustaining a legacy of excellence in innovation.

12.2.2 Enduring Resilience: Lessons from Challenges

Examine how Reliance Industries plans to navigate challenges in the long run. This subsection explores the lessons learned from past challenges and outlines strategies for enduring resilience in the face of future uncertainties.

12.3 The Global Impact of Mukesh Ambani's Legacy

12.3.1 Global Recognition and Contributions

Explore the global recognition garnered by Mukesh Ambani and Reliance Industries. This section examines the company's contributions to global development, its role in shaping international business standards, and the impact of Ambani's vision on a global scale.

12.3.2 Shaping Global Narratives: Ambani's Cultural and Economic Influence

Dive into how Mukesh Ambani's legacy contributes to shaping global narratives. From economic forums to cultural exchanges, this subsection explores how Ambani's influence endures in conversations about the intersection of business, culture, and society on a worldwide stage.

12.4 Mukesh Ambani's Philanthropic Endowment

12.4.1 Establishing a Philanthropic Legacy

Explore Ambani's philanthropic endowment and the establishment of a lasting legacy in societal development. This section unveils initiatives and foundations that will continue to contribute to education, healthcare, and community development in perpetuity.

12.4.2 Philanthropy Beyond a Lifetime

Examine how Mukesh Ambani envisions the continuation of philanthropic efforts beyond his lifetime. This subsection explores the strategies in place to ensure that Reliance Industries remains a philanthropic force, making a positive impact on communities for generations to come.

12.5 Mukesh Ambani's Reflections on a Storied Journey

12.5.1 A Personal Retrospective

As Chapter 12 draws to a close, the narrative shifts to Mukesh Ambani's personal reflections on a storied journey. This section provides insights into Ambani's reflections on leadership, legacy, and the enduring impact he aspires to leave on the world.

12.6 Symphony Unending: The Legacy Lives On

12.6.1 Mukesh Ambani's Lasting Impact

The final chapter concludes with a reflection on the enduring legacy of Mukesh Ambani. This section encapsulates the symphony unending, the legacy that lives on through Reliance Industries and the far-reaching impact of a visionary leader on the global stage.

"The Unending Symphony" not only captures the culmination of Mukesh Ambani's journey but sets the stage for the perpetual legacy of innovation, sustainability, and positive societal impact that will resonate for generations to come.

14

Summary

"Innovation Mogul: Mukesh Ambani's Impact on India's Corporate Landscape" is a comprehensive exploration of Mukesh Ambani's multifaceted influence on business, technology, society, and culture. The narrative spans 12 chapters, each unraveling a distinct facet of Ambani's journey and his imprint on Reliance Industries. From his early years and strategic business acumen to pioneering technological advancements and reshaping India's corporate landscape, Ambani emerges as a transformative leader.

Chapters 1 to 4 chart Ambani's rise in the corporate world, focusing on his strategic decisions, business ventures, and the disruptive entry of Reliance Jio into the telecommunications sector. Chapters 5 to 7 delve into Ambani's commitment to corporate social responsibility, his impact on education, healthcare, and rural development, and his pioneering role in technology. Chapter 8 propels the narrative into the future, exploring Ambani's vision for technological frontiers, e-commerce, and cutting-edge technologies.

Chapters 9 to 11 expand the scope to Ambani's impact on society, culture, and the global stage. The narrative unfolds Ambani's contributions to sports, philanthropy, media, and cultural diplomacy. It envisions Reliance Industries as a global force, influencing trade, technology, and cultural exchanges.

SUMMARY

Chapter 12 concludes the narrative, exploring Ambani's legacy, the perpetuity of Reliance Industries' impact, and Mukesh Ambani's reflections on a storied journey.

The symphony metaphor threads through the narrative, symbolizing the ongoing and enduring nature of Mukesh Ambani's influence. The biography captures the essence of Ambani's leadership, innovation, and commitment to societal progress, leaving a lasting imprint on the corporate and cultural landscape of India and the world.

www.ingramcontent.com/pod-product-compliance
Lightning Source LLC
LaVergne TN
LVHW012129070526
838202LV00056B/5931